Jenny Is Scared!

When Sad Things Happen
In The World

For Carter, and all of the world's innocents — CS
To my son, Seth — CP

Published by
MAGINATION PRESS
An Educational Publishing Foundation Book
American Psychological Association
750 First Street, NE
Washington, DC 20002

For more information about our books, including a complete catalog, please write to us, call 1-800-374-2721, or visit our website at www.maginationpress.com.

Editor: Darcie Conner Johnston
Art Director: Susan K. White
The text type is Excelsior
Printed by Phoenix Color, Rockaway, New Jersey

Library of Congress Cataloging-in-Publication Data

Shuman, Carol.
Jenny is scared : when sad things happen in the world / by Carol Shuman ;
illustrated by Cary Pillo.
p. cm.
Summary: When Jenny and her brother are frightened by events in the world, their parents help them talk about their fears and feel better.
ISBN 1-59147-002-1 (alk. paper) — ISBN 1-59147-003-X (pbk. : alk. paper)
1. Fear in children — Juvenile literature. [1. Fear. 2. Emotions.]
I. Pillo, Cary, ill. II. Title.
BF723.F4S58 2003
2002154980

Manufactured in the United States of America
10 9 8 7 6 5 4 3 2 1

Jenny Is Scared!

When Sad Things Happen
In The World

written by Carol Shuman

illustrated by Cary Pillo

MAGINATION PRESS • WASHINGTON, DC

My name is Jenny.
I have a big brother, Sam.
He says I get on his nerves sometimes
but that mostly I'm A-OK.
He makes me laugh a lot.

But today I am not laughing.
Today I am scared.

We didn't go to
school today.

Ms. Tina canceled
my piano lesson.

My friend Max
can't have his
birthday party.

Our TV shows aren't on.

Sam says that something bad happened.
Mom and Dad are watching a man on TV
who is talking about the bad thing.
Mom and Dad are being very quiet. They forgot
to make Sam and me lunch until we said we're hungry.

Sam says he is scared too.
I'm glad I have my brother to talk to.
It feels better to be scared together.
I know I am not the only one who
wonders what is happening.

9

We saw Mr. Lambert raking his leaves.
Sam asked him what is going on.
It's nothing for you kids to worry about, said Mr. Lambert.
But he looked worried, too!
We need to talk to Mom and Dad, I said.

What happened? we asked.
Mr. Lambert said not
to worry, but that just made
us more scared!

Mom hugged us.
Dad said that a lot of people are sad and worried.
Mom said that most of the time people do good
things in the world.
Most of the time the sun shines, the daisies grow,
and the skies are blue.
But sometimes sad things happen,
and sometimes people do bad things.

Dad said, When sad things happen we can talk to our moms and dads,

to our grandparents and aunts and uncles,

to our friends and neighbors,

to our teachers and counselors,

to our doctors and nurses,

to our cats and dogs and birds and hamsters,

and teddy bears,

and even to our goldfish if we have one.
Talking about our feelings makes us feel better.

I can talk about my feelings.
I am scared, I said. I don't want you to go out.
I don't want you to go anywhere without me.

Sam said, I don't want to hear about
the sad things on TV.
It makes me more scared.

I said, I am mad
because we can't
go to Max's party.

And I am sad because
I got mad and acted
grouchy to Max.

Sam said, I can't do my homework because I can only think about the bad thing. I forget what I am trying to read in my books.

We're both scared
that something else bad will happen!
We wish we could make it all go away.

18

Maybe if we cry really loud, the sad things will stop?

Or maybe if we are really good, or really quiet,

the bad things will stop?

Dad said, No, I'm afraid those things
won't make the sad things stop.
There will always be sad things.
But if we talk to each other and hug
each other a lot, we will
always feel better.

20

Mom said, You might have a little trouble
thinking in school for a little while.
You might have trouble listening
because you're thinking of other things.
But you'll be able to think better soon.

Dad said, We will also feel better
if we keep doing the things
we always do. That means I need
to play with my friends a lot,

do my chores,

go to school,

practice piano,

play soccer,

take baths
and go to bed
like always,

and eat lots of ice cream!

Mom said, It might help, too,
if we send some loving thoughts
to other people, because some
other people are not very happy.

I am still scared.
But I know that if I talk about how I feel,
then everybody will help me —
   my mom and dad,
      my brother,
         my grandparents and aunts and uncles,
            my friends,
               my teacher,
               my school counselor and school nurse,
            my doctor,
         my cat and my dog and my bird and my hamster,
      and my teddy bear,
and even my goldfish!

Dad said we can ask questions
if we want to know more.
I think sometimes I don't want to know more.
Dad said that's okay, too.

Sad things and bad things happen
sometimes, and I can't change that.
But it doesn't have to stop me from
playing in the sun,

and laughing
with my brother,

and going
to school,

and singing with
my friends,

and going to
birthday parties.

My mom and dad love me and my brother Sam.
I learned a big thing from the sad thing
that happened.
I learned that love is what matters.

If people love each other,
it's much better than when
people don't love each other.
It's love that helps us
through sad times and bad times
and mad times and any time.
I love all my family, and all the teachers,
and all my friends, and all the kids
in the world,

and all the sunshine,
and all the daisies,
and all the cats and dogs
and birds and hamsters
and teddy bears
and goldfish!

I love *the* whole world!
I hope you do too.

Note to Parents

BY ANN RASMUSSEN, PSY.D.

These are singularly difficult times to be parents and caregivers. When in America's history have children been so threatened by arbitrary and senseless danger, and when, therefore, have parents, teachers, and caregivers felt more helpless in their role as protectors? *Jenny Is Scared!* is a gentle tool for helping children cope with frightening national and world events. When working with children in the aftermath of sad or terrifying events, parents and caregivers are best equipped if they understand how children react to such traumatic events as war, terrorism, and natural disasters.

HOW CHILDREN REACT

Children are perceptive and imaginative. NOT discussing disturbing events tends to be more damaging and distressing to children than offering truthful (albeit appropriately tailored) explanation. Children's "littleness" and dependency on us for their very survival render them acutely sensitive to adult emotional states. Hushed voices, euphemisms, abruptly terminated conversations, and forced "everything's okay" tones all tell children that something is wrong. Even babies and toddlers perceive the tensions in their caretakers' eyes, facial expressions, holding behavior, and voices. Furthermore, saying nothing can be more damaging than telling the truth because children fill information voids with imaginings more terrifying than the reality. Thus, the "let's hide it from the children" option tends to heighten, not reduce, children's distress.

Children often have a more limited capacity than adults to tolerate painful feelings. As such, they may seem callous in their readiness to shift from upsetting news to superficial childhood concerns ("I feel bad that Sue's mom died. When do we eat?"). This may be a reflection of their inexperience with distressing life events and thus their unfamiliarity with how to sit with the feelings, make sense of them, give voice to them, find coping strategies for them, find solace for them, and so forth. Their processing style may be rather like a game of hot potato in which they furtively touch on painful feelings and questions, then swiftly get rid of the subject.

Thus, caregivers need to follow children's cues about the limits of their pain tolerance, as does Jenny's dad, who says it's okay that sometimes Jenny doesn't want to know more about the sad thing that happened. One should not assume children are done with a subject when they change it, however. Adults should remain attentive and receptive to further discussion and comforting as needed, over a long period of time. Related fears, sleep and eating disturbances, and delayed or monthly or yearly anniversary reactions may signal continued underlying struggle and need for help. By following such cues, caregivers can slowly cultivate the emotional skills and coping strategies that will stand children in good stead when facing the hardships of life to come.

Children express in other ways what they can't verbalize. Because children possess limited vocabulary and coping skills for painful feelings, they are more prone to express their distress symptomatically— through behavior and physiological complaints. Children's tendency toward symptom formation is in direct proportion to their inability to articulate their feelings. Furthermore, stress in a child's environment can prompt him or her to regress to a safer position of old, when the child was younger and less self-reliant. A frightened child might be clingy and refuse to separate from parents, or return to bedwetting or thumb sucking, or avoid taking on new challenges formerly anticipated happily. Emotional unease, if hard to voice, may be expressed as physiological unease in the form of stomachaches, fatigue, headaches, and agitation. These aches and pains have the added benefit of enlisting extra tender loving care from parents, which is so vitally needed psychologically.

Our job as caretakers is to remain mindful of the larger distressing context and to help the child understand these symptoms. A parent might say, "I'm so sorry your stomach is hurting this morning. I'll help it feel better, don't worry. I wonder if also you feel sick to your stomach about the bad news we heard last night about the plane crash. I'm feeling that way myself today." Remaining mindful of the larger context for the child also means considering what past stresses or losses are reawakened by the current distress. For example, a child whose

parents just divorced may be more wobbly coping with a fresh loss because of a continued feeling of insecure footing in the world.

Needless to say, if symptoms persist and medical causes have been ruled out, consider obtaining counseling for the child.

Children feel personally endangered far more readily than do adults. This is because children see the world from a more self-centered vantage point (in the cognitive, not moral, sense) until they are well into their teens. For example, a child's first reflexive thoughts in learning of a friend's illness may not be, "Poor Alex, is he in pain? How might I help?" but instead, "Is it catching? Did I get it by using his pillow on the overnight? Can he still come to my birthday party?" Similarly, large-scale crises may evoke highly personalized fears: "Will a kidnapper come into my window? Will a sniper come to my playground? Will the enemy attack our neighborhood? Will Mommy's plane crash too?" Therefore, it is vital to ferret out what fantastical fear children have dreamed up so that you can disabuse them of these notions.

Children are literal and concrete thinkers. Children's immature language skills necessitate simple, concrete, and limited explanations by adults. Children's lack of abstract reasoning capacity makes them at risk for misconstruing adult's figures of speech, and the resulting potential for confusion and alarm is considerable. For example, "Grandma is sleeping with the angels" could invoke fears about dying while asleep or feelings of resentful rejection that Grandma couldn't have stayed on earth to rest right here in the guest bed where she seemed perfectly happy. References to "resting" or "passing on" befuddle children, as they know people finally get enough rest and wake up, or that passing on doesn't necessarily mean they can't pass on back. Children can get caught up waiting interminably rather than coming to terms with the finality of their loss.

HOW PARENTS CAN HELP

Be honest. Response to children's questions with an open mind and heart, unobstructed by attempts to hide the truth "for their own good." Of course, you won't want to divulge horrifying details, only the information that you believe your child can make use of, depending on his or her maturity and need to know. Honesty is ultimately reassuring to chil-

dren. An added benefit is that you teach them the value of respectful forthrightness.

Listen openly and respectfully. Summary dismissal of sad, anxious, or mad feelings as "silly" teaches children to hide their most difficult feelings in the most vulnerable of times, and from those adults who are supposed to be their closest caregivers. What might seem ludicrous concerns to adults may evolve into disturbing terrors if allowed to fester. In contrast, an attitude of respectful concern teaches children that people are valuable resources to turn to for care and help at critical times in life. Such a lesson will stand them in good stead all their years.

Find out what they know. Ferret out misconceptions that children harbor before answering questions. Ask, "What have you heard already? How do you think it happened? Tell me the worries you have about what else might happen?" Adults can't disabuse children of fantastical or distorted notions unless they elicit them in the first place.

Use simple words. Speak in words of single syllables to explain what happened. For example: "Some boys who were really mad about their lives and were filled up with hate went wild and shot guns at people at their school. The police got them right away and put them in jail. They can't hurt anyone now. The doctors are helping the shot people get better as best they can."

Put events in context. Embed the stressful event in a reassuring framework to stop alarm and despair from overtaking a child's perspective. Emphasize ways that the danger is rare (e.g., "thousands of planes take off and land every day without a single problem"); that everything is being done to prevent its reoccurrence (e.g., "we have the most powerful military forces in the world to protect us every hour of every day"); and that children are well protected and loved by their caregivers (e.g., "we keep our house safe with our doors and windows locked, and we know how to call 911 to bring the police right away. And I'm sure you know by now that the most important job for me, besides loving you, is keeping you safe, always.")

Find the good. Seek out and celebrate instances of heroism, resourcefulness, resilience, kindness, and generosity shown by people in the midst of sad or scary events. Children can learn the value of valiant honor over helpless surrender when faced with frightening life circumstances.

Minimize media exposure. Monitor and restrict news exposure to avoid subjecting children to frightening images depicted via TV, computer, radio, and newspaper. Such coverage can assault children (and adults as well) with gratuitous, gory details that themselves traumatize and compound the recovery process.

Foster children's spiritual lives. Draw on and educate children about religious or spiritual frameworks that might help temper fear and despair. Life's cruelest hardships offer pivotal opportunities to nourish hope-inspiring spiritual growth in us and in our children.

Get involved. Support community outreach activities to combat a sense of helpless passivity. Enlisting children to brainstorm ways to ease victims' hardship may yield creative and useful ways to shift children from the position of impotent vulnerability to altruistic agency. Examples include collecting clothes for families rendered homeless by fire, making energy-sustaining treats for local heroes, making mobiles of drawings and messages to hang over hospitalized victims' heads, participating in myriad ways with relief agencies, sending extra books and school supplies to students displaced by violence or natural disaster, and so on.

Focus on routines and relating. Maintain routines, minimize stress, and maximize loving family time. The more stress there is in the environment, the more everyone needs the comfort of simple routines and the rejuvenating joys of companionship with those closest to us. Life's cruelties drain our emotional reservoirs. We restore our strength and buoyancy through creative and loving connections that counterbalance life's hardships and remind us of our blessings. As Jenny says, "Sad things and bad things happen sometimes, and I can't change that. But it doesn't have to stop me from playing in the sun. I learned a big thing from the sad thing that happened. I learned that love is what matters."

Ann Rasmussen, Psy.D., is a clinical psychologist, psychotherapist, author, and public speaker. She lives in Montclair, New Jersey, with her husband and three children.

About the Author

CAROL SHUMAN, PH.D., is a clinical psychologist with a specialty in behavioral medicine. As a psychotherapist, she works with children, adolescents, and adults. She is also a university teacher, registered nurse, public speaker, and newspaper columnist. She lives in Bermuda. *Jenny Is Scared!* is her first book for children.

About the Illustrator

CARY PILLO grew up on a farm near the Cascade Mountains in Washington State, and began drawing at an early age. She is the illustrator of several children's books, including *A Terrible Thing Happened* and *Tibby Tried It*, and her colorful characters appear in many children's magazines as well. She lives in Seattle with her husband and son, and their dog Rocket.